Vegan Mediterranean Coo
Incredibly Delicious Vegan Salad, S
and Skillet Recipes from the Mediterranean Diet

by **Vesela Tabakova**
Text copyright(c)2013 Vesela Tabakova

Table Of Contents

Eating the Mediterranean Diet as a Vegan

The Mediterranean way of life is relaxed and family-oriented. Living, cooking and eating are joyous, shared activities. In the Mediterranean countries eating means sharing food and conversation with someone. And cooking means preparing delicious meals for your family and friends, so you can all gather around the table and enjoy food together. A fundamental characteristic of Mediterranean cuisine is that food is cooked using easily available ingredients - local, everyday products that we can buy around the corner or grow in our own backyard, therefore, it's easy enough to veganize the Mediterranean diet, bringing a more sustainable and compassionate quality to this style of eating.

My family favorite vegan Mediterranean dishes are easy to prepare and delicious because they include olive oil, fresh, seasonal, locally grown vegetables, protein-rich legumes and whole grains, nuts, seeds, and aromatic, superfood herbs and spices. My vegan meals are generally prepared slowly and simply, all in one pot, very rarely deep fried.

The health benefits of the Mediterranean diet are well known, proven with research, and hard to ignore. It is rightly considered the best plant-based diet in the world and switching to a Mediterranean diet will help you enjoy an active long life, will greatly improve your health and beauty, and even your mood.

Salads and Appetizers

Greek Chickpea Salad

Serves 4-5

Ingredients:

1 cup canned chickpeas, drained and rinsed

1-2 spring onions, thinly sliced

1 small cucumber, peeled and diced

2 green bell peppers, diced

2 tomatoes, diced

2 tsp chopped fresh parsley

1 tsp capers, drained and rinsed

juice of 1/2 lemon

2 tbsp olive oil

1 tsp balsamic vinegar

salt and pepper, to taste

a pinch of dried oregano

Directions:

In a medium bowl, toss together the chickpeas, green onion, cucumber, bell pepper, tomato, parsley, capers, and lemon juice.

In a smaller bowl, stir together the remaining ingredients and pour over the chickpea salad.

Toss well to coat and allow to marinate, stirring occasionally, for at least 1 hour before serving.

The Best Orzo Salad

Serves 6

Ingredients:

For the dressing:

1/3 cup extra-virgin olive oil

3/4 cup fresh lemon juice

1 tbsp dried mint

For the salad:

9 oz uncooked orzo

2 tbsp olive oil

a bunch of spring onions, chopped

½ cup chopped green peppers

½ cup stoneless black olives, cut

1 cup fresh tomatoes, diced

1 cup roasted sunflower seeds

Directions:

The dressing:

Combine the olive oil, lemon juice, and mint in a small bowl, mixing well. Place the dressing in the refrigerator until ready to use.

Cook the orzo according to package directions (in salted water) and rinse thoroughly with cold water when you strain it. Transfer to a large bowl and toss with the olive oil.

Allow orzo to cool completely. Once orzo is cooled, add the diced peppers, finely cut spring onions, olives and diced tomatoes stirring until mixed well.

Stir the dressing (it will have separated by this point) and add it to the salad, tossing to evenly coat. Add salt and pepper to taste and sprinkle with roasted sunflower seeds.

Kale Salad with Creamy Tahini Dressing

Serves 4

Ingredients:

1 head kale

2 cucumbers, peeled and diced

1 avocado, peeled and diced

1 red onion, finely chopped

1 cup cherry tomatoes, halved

for the dressing

1/3 cup tahini

1/2 cup water

2 garlic cloves, minced

3 tbsp lemon juice

4 tbsp olive oil

salt and freshly ground black pepper, to taste

Directions:

Prepare the dressing by whisking all ingredients.

Place all salad ingredients in bowl and toss with the dressing.

Season to taste with black pepper and salt and serve.

Tabbouleh

Serves 6

Ingredients:

1 cup raw bulgur

2 cups boiling water

a bunch of parsley, finely cut

2 tomatoes, chopped

3 tbsp olive oil

2 garlic cloves, minced

6-7 spring, chopped

1 tbsp fresh mint leaves, chopped

juice of two lemons

salt and black pepper, to taste

Directions:

Bring water and salt to a boil, then pour over bulgur. Cover and set aside for 15 minutes to steam. Drain excess water and fluff with a fork.

In a large bowl, mix together the parsley, tomatoes, olive oil, garlic, spring onions and mint.

Stir in the chilled bulgur and season to taste with salt, pepper and lemon juice.

Fatoush

Serves 5-6

Ingredients:

2 cups green lettuce, finely chopped

2 ripe tomatoes, diced

1 cucumber, peeled and chopped

1 green pepper, seeded and chopped

1 cup radishes, sliced

1 small red onion, finely chopped

1/2 cup parsley, finely cut

2 tbsp finely chopped fresh mint

3 tbsp olive oil

4 tbsp lemon juice

salt and black pepper, to taste

2 whole-wheat pita breads

Directions:

Toast the pita breads in a skillet until they are browned and crisp. Set aside.

Place the lettuce, tomatoes, cucumbers, green pepper, radishes, onion, parsley and mint in a salad bowl. Break up the toasted pita into bite-size pieces and add to the salad.

Make the dressing by whisking together the olive oil with the lemon juice, a pinch of salt and some black pepper. Toss together until everything is coated with the dressing and serve.

Fried Zucchinis with Tomato Sauce

Serves 4

Ingredients:

4 zucchinis medium size, peeled and sliced

1 cup flour

For the tomato sauce

4-5 ripe tomatoes, skinned and grated

1 carrot

½ onion

2 cloves garlic, whole

1 tsp salt

11/2 cup sunflower oil

1 tsp sugar

1/2 cup parsley, finely cut

Directions:

Wash and peel the zucchinis, and cut them in thin diagonal slices or in rings. Sprinkle with salt and leave aside in a suitable bowl placing it inclined to drain away the juices.

Coat the zucchinis with flour, then fry, turning on both sides, until they are golden-brown (about 3 minutes on each side). Transfer to paper towels and pat dry.

Heat the oil in a large skillet and cook the onion and the carrot until soft. Add the grated tomatoes together with two whole garlic cloves. Season with salt and half a teaspoon of sugar. Simmer at low heath until thick and ready. Sprinkle with parsley and pour over the fried zucchinis.

Brown Lentil Salad

Serves 4

Ingredients:

1 can lentils, drained and rinsed

1 red onion, thinly sliced

1 tomato, diced

1 red bell pepper, chopped

2 garlic cloves, crushed

2 tbsp lemon juice

1/3 cup parsley leaves, finely cut

salt and pepper, to taste

Directions:

Place the lentils, red onion, tomato, bell pepper, and lemon juice in a large bowl. Season with salt and black pepper to taste.

Toss to combine, sprinkle with parsley and serve.

Beetroot Salad

Serves 4

Ingredients:

2-3 small beets, peeled

3-4 spring onions, chopped

3 cloves garlic, pressed

2 tbsp red wine vinegar

2-3 tbsp sunflower oil

salt, to taste

Directions:

Place the beats in a steam basket set over a pot of boiling water. Steam for about 12-15 minutes or until tender. Leave to cool.

Grate the beets and put them in a salad bowl. Add the crushed garlic cloves, the finely cut onions and mix well.

Season with salt, vinegar and sunflower oil.

Spinach Stem Salad

Serves 1-2

Ingredients:

a few bunches of spinach stems

water to boil the stems

1 garlic clove, crushed

lemon juice or vinegar, to taste

3 tbsp olive oil

salt, to taste

Directions:

Trim the stems so that they remain whole. Wash them very well. Steam them in a basket over boiling water for 2 to 3 minutes, until wilted but not too soft.

Place the spinach stems on a plate and sprinkle with crushed garlic, olive oil, lemon juice or vinegar, and salt.

Spring Green Salad

Serves 4

Ingredients:

1 head of lettuce, washed and drained

1 cucumber, peeled and cut

8-9 radishes

4-5 spring onions

the juice of half a lemon or 2 tbsp of white wine vinegar

3 tbsp sunflower or olive oil

salt, to taste

Directions:

Cut the lettuce into thin strips. Slice the cucumber and the radishes as thinly as possible and chop the green onions.

Mix all the salad ingredients in a large bowl, add the lemon juice and oil and season with salt to taste.

Roasted Vegetable Salad

Serves 4

Ingredients:

2 tomatoes, halved

1 medium zucchini, quartered

1 eggplant, ends trimmed, quartered

2 large red pepper, halved, deseeded, cut into strips

2-3 white button mushrooms, halved

1 onion, quartered

1 tsp garlic powder

2 tbsp olive oil

for the dressing:

1 tbsp lemon juice

1 tbsp apple cider vinegar

2 tbsp olive oil

1 tsp sumac

5 tbsp crushed walnuts, to serve

Directions:

Whisk olive oil, lemon juice, vinegar and sumac in a bowl.

Preheat oven to 500 F. Place the zucchini, eggplant, peppers, onion, mushrooms and tomatoes on a lined baking sheet. Sprinkle with olive oil, season with salt, pepper and sumac and roast until golden, about 25 minutes. Divide in 4-5 plates, top with crushed walnuts, drizzle with the dressing and serve.

Beet and Bean Sprout Salad

Serves 4

Ingredients:

7 beet greens, finely sliced

2 medium tomatoes, sliced

1 cup bean sprouts, washed

1 tbsp grated lemon rind

2 garlic cloves, crushed

1/4 cup lemon juice

1/4 cup olive oil

1 tsp salt

Directions:

In a large bowl, toss together beet greens, bean sprouts, tomatoes, and dressing.

Mix oil and lemon juice with lemon rind, salt and garlic and pour over the salad.

Refrigerate for 2 hours to allow flavor to develop before serving. Serve chilled.

Easy White Bean Salad

Serves: 4-5

Ingredients:

9 oz white beans

1 yellow onion

1 red onion, chopped

3 tbsp white vinegar

a bunch of fresh parsley

salt and black pepper, to taste

Directions:

Wash the beans and soak them in cold water to swell overnight. Cook in the same water with the yellow onion. When tender, drain and put into a deeper bowl. Remove the onion.

Mix well oil, vinegar, salt and pepper. Pour over still warm beans, leave to cool about 30-40 minutes.

Chop the red onion and the parsley, add to the beans, mix and serve.

Winter Cabbage Salad

Serves 4

Ingredients:

9 oz fresh white cabbage, shredded

9 oz carrots, shredded

9 oz white turnips, shredded

½ a bunch of parsley

2 tbsp white vinegar

3 tbsp sunflower oil

salt, to taste

Directions:

Combine first three ingredients in a large bowl and stir to combine.

Add in salt, vinegar and oil. Stir and sprinkle with parsley.

Roasted Peppers with Garlic and Parsley

Serves 4-6

Ingredients:

2 lb red and green bell peppers

1/2 cup sunflower oil

5-6 tbsp white vinegar

3-4 cloves garlic, chopped

a small bunch of fresh parsley

salt and pepper, to taste

Directions:

Grill the peppers or roast them in the oven at 400 F until the skins are a little burnt. Place the roasted peppers in a brown paper bag or a lidded container and leave covered for about 10 minutes. This makes it easier to peel them. Peel the skins and remove the seeds.

Cut the peppers into strips lengthwise and layer them in a bowl. Mix together the oil, vinegar, salt and pepper, chopped garlic and the chopped parsley leaves. Pour over the peppers.

Cover the roasted peppers and chill for an hour.

Cucumber Salad

Serves 4

Ingredients:

2 medium cucumbers, sliced

a bunch of fresh dill

2 cloves garlic

3 tbsp white wine vinegar

5 tbsp olive oil

salt, to taste

Directions:

Cut the cucumbers in rings and put them in a salad bowl.

Add the finely cut dill, the pressed garlic and season with salt, vinegar and oil.

Mix well and serve cold.

Baby Spinach Salad

Serves 4

Ingredients:

1 bag baby spinach, washed and dried

1 red bell pepper, cut in slices

1 cup cherry tomatoes, cut in halves

1 red onion, finely chopped

1 cup black olives, pitted

1 tsp dried oregano

1 large garlic clove

3 tbsp red wine vinegar

4 tbsp olive oil

salt and freshly ground black pepper, to taste

Directions:

Prepare the dressing by blending the garlic and the oregano with the olive oil and the vinegar in a food processor.

Place the spinach leaves in a large salad bowl and toss with the dressing. Add the rest of the ingredients and give everything a toss again. Season to taste with black pepper and salt.

Mediterranean Buckwheat Salad

Serves 4-5

Ingredients:

1 cup buckwheat groats

1 3/4 cups water

1 small red onion, finely chopped

1/2 cucumber, diced

1 cup cherry tomatoes, halved

1 yellow bell pepper, chopped

a bunch of parsley, finely cut

1 preserved lemon, finely chopped

1 cup chickpeas, cooked or canned, drained

juice of half lemon

1 tsp dried basil

2 tbsp olive oil

salt and black pepper, to taste

Directions:

Heat a large, dry saucepan and toast the buckwheat for about three minutes. Boil the water and add it carefully to the buckwheat. Cover, reduce heat and simmer until buckwheat is tender and all liquid is absorbed (5-7 minutes). Remove from heat, fluff with a fork and set aside to cool.

Mix the buckwheat with the chopped onion, bell pepper, cucumber, cherry tomatoes, parsley, preserved lemon and chickpeas in a salad bowl.

Whisk the lemon juice, olive oil and basil, season with salt and pepper to taste, then pour over the salad and stir. Serve at room temperature.

Spicy Buckwheat Vegetable Salad

Serves 4-5

Ingredients:

1 cup buckwheat groats

2 cups vegetable broth

2 tomatoes, diced

1/2 cup green onions, chopped

1/2 cup parsley leaves, finely chopped

1/2 cup fresh mint leaves, very finely chopped

1/2 yellow bell pepper, chopped

1 cucumber, peeled and cut into 1/4-inch cubes

1/2 cup cooked or canned brown lentils, drained

1/4 cup freshly squeezed lemon juice

1 tsp hot pepper sauce

Directions:

Heat a large, dry saucepan and toast the buckwheat for about three minutes. Boil the vegetable broth and add it carefully to the buckwheat. Cover, reduce heat and simmer until buckwheat is tender and all liquid is absorbed (five-seven minutes).

Remove from heat, fluff with a fork and set aside to cool.

Chop all vegetables and add them together with the lentils to the buckwheat.

Mix the lemon juice and remaining ingredients well and drizzle over the buckwheat mixture. Stir well to distribute the dressing evenly.

Buckwheat Salad with Asparagus and Roasted Peppers

Serves 4-5

Ingredients:

1 cup buckwheat groats

1 3/4 cups vegetable broth

1/2 lb asparagus, trimmed and cut into 1 inch pieces

4 roasted red bell peppers, peeled and diced

2-3 spring onions, finely chopped

2 garlic cloves, crushed

1 tbsp red wine vinegar

3 tbsp olive oil

1/2 cup fresh parsley leaves, finely cut

Directions:

Heat a large dry saucepan and toast the buckwheat for about three minutes. Boil the vegetable broth and add it carefully to the buckwheat. Cover, reduce heat and simmer until buckwheat is tender and all liquid is absorbed (five-seven minutes).

Remove from heat, fluff with a fork and set aside to cool.

Rinse out the saucepan and bring about an inch of water to a boil. Cook the asparagus in a steamer basket or colander, 2-3 minutes until tender. Transfer the asparagus in a large bowl along with the roasted peppers. Add in the spring onions, garlic, red wine vinegar, salt, pepper and olive oil. Stir to combine.

Add the buckwheat to the vegetable mixture. Sprinkle with parsley and toss the salad gently. Serve at room temperature.

Artichoke and Bean Salad with Lemon Mint Dressing

Serves 5

Ingredients:

1 can white beans, drained

2/3 cup podded broad beans

4 marinated artichoke hearts, quartered

2/3 cup diced green bell pepper

for the dressing:

3 tbsp olive oil

3 tbsp lemon juice

1 tsp dried mint

5-6 fresh mint leaves, very finely cut

salt and pepper, to taste

Boil the broad beans in unsalted water for 3-4 minutes or until tender. Drain and hold under running cold water for a few minutes. Combine with the canned beans, bell peppers and quartered marinated artichoke hearts in a deep salad bowl.

In a small bowl, mix olive oil, lemon juice, dried mint and fresh mint. Whisk until smooth. Add in salt and pepper and pour over salad. Toss gently to combine and serve.

Artichoke and Mushroom Salad

Serves: 4-5

Ingredients:

1 oz can artichoke hearts, drained, cut quartered

7-8 white button mushrooms, chopped

1 red pepper, chopped

1/3 cup chopped black olives

1 tbsp capers

3 tbsp lemon juice

2 tbsp olive oil

salt and pepper, to taste

Directions:

Place the artichokes and mushrooms in a large salad bowl and stir to mix well. Add in olives, capers and red pepper and toss to combine.

In a small bowl, whisk the lemon juice and olive oil until smooth. Pour over the salad, toss and serve.

Green Bean and Radicchio Salad with Green Olive Dressing

Serves: 4

Ingredients:

1 lb trimmed green beans, cut to 2-3 inch long pieces

1 radicchio, outer leaves removed, washed, dried

1 small red onion, finely cut

1 cup cherry tomatoes, halved

green olive dressing

1/2 cup green olives, pitted

1/2 cup olive oil

2 garlic cloves, chopped

black pepper and salt, to taste

Directions:

Roughly tear the radicchio leaves and place on a large serving platter.

Steam or boil green beans for about 3-4 minutes until crisp-tender. In a colander, wash with cold water to stop cooking, then pat dry and arrange over the radicchio leaves.

Add in red onion and cherry tomatoes.

To make the green olive dressing, place the olives in a food processor and blend until finely chopped. Gradually add the oil and process until a smooth paste is formed. Taste and season with salt and pepper then spoon over salad and serve.

Okra Salad

Serves 4

Ingredients:

1.2 lb young okras

1 lemon

½ bunch parsley, chopped

2 tomatoes, sliced

for the dressing:

3 tbsp sunflower oil

½ tsp black pepper

salt, to taste

Directions:

Trim okras, then wash and cook them in salted water until tender. Drain and set aside to cool.

In a small bowl mix well the lemon juice and sunflower oil, salt and black pepper.

Arrange okra and tomatoes in a bowl then pour over the dressing and sprinkle with chopped parsley.

Soups

Spiced Root Soup

Serves 4

Prep time: 30 min

Ingredients:

2 parsnips, peeled, chopped

2 leeks, chopped

2 carrots, chopped

1 potato, peeled and diced

4 cups vegetable broth

1/2 cup almond milk

1 garlic clove

3 tbsp olive oil

1 tbsp curry powder

1/2 tsp cumin

salt and freshly ground pepper, to taste

Directions:

Heat olive oil in a large saucepan and sauté the leeks and garlic together with the curry powder and cumin. Stir in the parsnips, carrot and potato and cook, stirring often, for 10 minutes.

Add the vegetable broth, bring to the boil, and simmer for 20 minutes, or until the vegetables are tender.

Set aside to cool then blend in batches until smooth. Return soup to pan over low heat and stir in the almond milk. Season with salt and black pepper to taste.

Creamy Red Lentil Soup

Serves: 4

Prep time: 30 min

Ingredients:

1 cup red lentils

1/2 small onion, chopped

1 garlic clove, chopped

1 red pepper, chopped

3 cups water

1 can coconut milk

3 tbsp olive oil

1 tsp paprika

1/2 tsp ginger

salt and black pepper, to taste

Directions:

Heat olive oil in a large saucepan and sauté onion, garlic, red pepper, paprika, ginger and cumin, stirring.

Add in red lentils and water. Bring to a boil, cover, and simmer for 20 minutes. Add in coconut milk and simmer for 5 more minutes.

Remove from heat, season with salt and black pepper, and blend until smooth.

Creamy Celery Soup

Serves: 4

Prep time: 30 min

Ingredients:

2 cups chopped celery ribs or celeriac

1 potato, peeled and diced

1/2 small onion, chopped

1 garlic clove, crushed

3 cups vegetable broth

1 cup almond milk

1 tbsp fresh dill, finely cut

3 tbsp olive oil

salt and black pepper, to taste

Directions:

Heat olive oil over medium-high heat and sauté onion, garlic, celery and potato for 3-4 minutes, stirring. Add in vegetable broth.

Bring to a boil then reduce heat and simmer, covered, for 20 minutes. Stir in the almond milk and dill and blend until smooth.

Return soup to the pot and cook over medium-high heat until heated through. Season with salt and black pepper to taste and serve.

Moroccan Lentil Soup

Serves 10

Ingredients:

1 cup red lentils

1 cup canned chickpeas, drained

2 onions, chopped

2 cloves garlic, minced

1 cup canned tomatoes, chopped

1 cup canned white beans, drained

3 carrots, diced

3 celery ribs, diced

4 cups water

1 tsp ginger, grated

1 tsp ground cardamom

1/2 tsp cumin

3 tbsp olive oil

Directions:

In a large pot, sauté onions, garlic and ginger in olive oil for about 5 minutes. Add the water, lentils, chickpeas, white beans, tomatoes, carrots, celery, cardamom and cumin.

Bring to a boil for a few minutes, then simmer for half an hour or longer until the lentils are tender. Puree half the soup in a food processor or blender. Return the pureed soup to the pot, stir and serve.

Italian Minestrone

Serves 4-5

Ingredients:

¼ cabbage, chopped

2 carrots, chopped

1 celery rib, thinly sliced

1 small onion, chopped

2 garlic cloves, chopped

2 tbsp olive oil

3 cups water

1 cup canned tomatoes, diced, undrained

1 cup fresh spinach, torn

1/2 cup pasta, cooked

black pepper and salt, to taste

Directions:

Sauté the carrots, cabbage, celery, onion and garlic in oil for 5 minutes in a deep saucepan. Add water, tomatoes and bring to a boil.

Reduce heat and simmer uncovered, for 20 minutes, or until vegetables are tender. Stir in spinach, macaroni, and season with pepper and salt to taste.

French Vegetable Soup

Serves 6

Ingredients:

1 leek, thinly sliced

1 large zucchini, peeled and diced

1 cup green beans, cut

2 garlic cloves, cut

3 cups vegetable broth

1 cup canned tomatoes, chopped

3.5 oz vermicelli, broken into small pieces

3 tbsp olive oil

black pepper, to taste

Directions:

Sauté the leek, zucchini, green beans and garlic for about 5 minutes. Add the vegetable broth. Stir in the tomatoes and bring to the boil then reduce heat.

Add black pepper to taste and simmer for 10 minutes or until the vegetables are tender but still holding their shape. Stir in the vermicelli. Cover again and simmer for a further 5 minutes. Serve warm.

Roasted Brussels Sprouts and Cauliflower Soup

Serves 4

Ingredients:

1 onion, finely chopped

2 garlic cloves, crushed

16 oz cauliflower florets

16 oz Brussels sprouts, halved

4 cups vegetable broth

6 tbsp olive oil

salt and pepper, to taste

Directions:

Preheat oven to 450F.

Line a large baking sheet and place the cauliflower and Brussels sprouts on it. Drizzle with half the olive oil and roast on the bottom third of the oven for 30 minutes, or until slightly browned.

Heat the remaining oil in a saucepan over medium heat and sauté the onion and garlic, stirring, for 2-3 minutes or until soft.

Add in vegetable broth and bring to the boil then simmer 3-4 minutes. Stir in roasted vegetables and cook for 5 minutes more.

Set aside to cool then blend in batches and reheat.

Beetroot and Carrot Soup

Serves 5-6

Ingredients:

4 beets, washed and peeled

2 carrots, peeled, chopped

2 potatoes, peeled, chopped

1 medium onion, chopped

2 cups vegetable broth

2 cups water

2 tbsp olive oil

a bunch of spring onions, cut, to serve

Directions:

Peel and chop the beets. Heat olive oil in a saucepan over medium high heat and sauté onion and carrot until onion is tender. Add beets, potatoes, broth and water. Bring to the boil. Reduce heat to medium and simmer, partially covered, for 30-40 minutes, or until beets are tender. Cool slightly.

Blend soup in batches until smooth. Return it to pan over low heat and cook, stirring, for 4-5 minutes, or until heated through. Season with salt and pepper. Serve sprinkled with spring onions.

Monastery Style White Bean Soup

Serves 6

Ingredients:

9 oz white beans

2-3 carrots

2 onions, finely chopped

1-2 tomatoes, grated

1 red bell pepper, chopped

4-5 springs of fresh mint and parsley

1 tsp paprika

¼ cup sunflower oil

salt, to taste

Directions:

Soak the beans in cold water for 3-4 hours, drain and discard the water. Cover the beans with cold water.

Add the oil, finely chopped carrots, onions and pepper. Bring to the boil and simmer until the beans are tender.

Add the grated tomatoes, mint, paprika and salt. Simmer for another 15 minutes.

Serve sprinkled with finely chopped parsley.

Cream-less Cauliflower Soup

Serves 5-6

Ingredients:

¼ cup olive oil

1 large onion, finely cut

1 medium head cauliflower, chopped

2-3 garlic cloves, minced

3 cups vegetable broth

salt, to taste

fresh ground black pepper, to taste

Directions:

Heat the olive oil in a large pot over medium heat and gently sauté the onion, cauliflower and garlic.

Stir in the vegetable broth and bring the mixture to a boil.

Reduce heat, cover, and simmer for 30 minutes. Remove the soup from heat and blend in a blender or with a hand mixer. Season with salt and pepper and serve.

Pumpkin and Bell Pepper Soup

Serves 4

Ingredients:

1 medium leek, chopped

9 oz pumpkin, peeled, deseeded, cut into small cubes

1/2 small red pepper, cut into small pieces

1 can tomatoes, undrained, crushed

3 cups vegetable broth

1/2 tsp cumin

salt and black pepper, to taste

Directions:

Heat the olive oil in a medium saucepan and sauté the leek for 4-5 minutes. Add the pumpkin and bell pepper and cook, stirring, for 5 minutes. Add tomatoes, broth, and cumin and bring to the boil.

Cover, reduce heat to low and simmer, stirring occasionally, for 30 minute,s or until vegetables are soft. Season with salt and pepper and leave aside to cool. Blend in batches and re-heat to serve.

Mushroom Soup

Serves 4

Ingredients:

1 lb white button mushrooms, peeled and chopped

1 onion, chopped

2 cloves of garlic, crushed

1 tsp thyme

3 cups vegetable broth

salt and pepper, to taste

3 tbsp olive oil

Directions:

Sauté onions and garlic in a large soup pot until transparent. Add thyme and mushrooms.

Stir and cook for 10 minutes, then add the vegetable broth and simmer for another 10-20 minutes. Blend, season and serve.

Spinach Soup

Serves 4

Ingredients:

14 oz frozen spinach

1 large onion or 4-5 spring onions

1 carrot

3-4 tbsp olive or sunflower oil

1/4 cup white rice

1-2 cloves garlic, cut

1 tsp paprika

black pepper, to taste

salt, to taste

Directions:

Heat oil in a cooking pot. Add the onion and carrot and sauté together for a few minutes, until just softened. Add chopped garlic, paprika and rice and stir for a minute. Remove from heat.

Add the spinach along with about 3 cups of hot water and season with salt and pepper. Bring back to the boil, then reduce the heat and simmer for around 30 minutes.

Nettle Soup

Serves 4

Ingredients:

1.2 lb young top shoots of nettles, well washed

3-4 tbsp sunflower oil

2 potatoes, diced small

1 bunch of green onions, coarsely chopped

2 cups hot water

1 tsp salt

Directions:

Clean the young nettles, wash and cook them in slightly salted water. Drain, rinse, drain again and then chop or pass through a sieve.

Sauté the chopped green onions and potatoes in the oil until the potatoes start to color a little.

Turn off the heat, add the nettles, then gradually stir in the water. Stir well, then simmer until the potatoes are cooked through.

Pumpkin and Chickpea Soup

Serves 6

Ingredients:

1 leek, white part only, thinly sliced

3 cloves garlic, finely chopped

2 carrots, peeled, coarsely chopped

2 lb pumpkin, peeled, deseeded, diced

1/3 cup chickpeas

½ tsp ground ginger

½ tsp ground cinnamon

½ tsp ground cumin

5 tbsp olive oil

Juice of ½ lemon

parsley springs, to serve

Directions:

Heat oil in a large saucepan and sauté leek, garlic and 2 tsp salt, stirring occasionally, until soft. Add cinnamon, ginger and cumin and stir. Add in carrots, pumpkin and chickpeas.

Add 5 cups of water to saucepan and bring to the boil, then reduce heat and simmer for 50 minutes or until the chickpeas are soft.

Remove from heat, add lemon juice and blend soup, in batches, until smooth. Return it to pan over low heat and cook, stirring, for 4-5 minutes, or until heated through. Serve topped with parsley sprigs.

Brussels Sprout and Potato Soup

Serves 4-5

Ingredients:

16 oz Brussels sprouts

2 potatoes, peeled and chopped

1 onion, chopped

3 garlic cloves, crushed

4 cups water

2 tbsp olive oil

salt and black pepper, to taste

Directions:

Heat oil in a large saucepan over medium-high heat. Add onion and garlic and sauté, stirring, for 1-2 minutes until fragrant.

Add in Brussels sprouts, potatoes, rosemary and 4 cups of vegetable broth.

Cover and bring to the boil, then reduce heat to low. Simmer for 30 minutes, or until potatoes are tender.

Remove from heat. Blend until smooth. Return to pan. Cook for 4-5 minutes or until heated through. Season with salt and pepper and serve.

Brussels Sprout and Tomato Soup

Serves 4-5

Ingredients:

16 oz Brussels sprouts

4 large tomatoes, diced

1 medium onion, chopped

3 garlic cloves, crushed

1 tsp sugar

2 cups vegetable broth

1 tbsp paprika

2 tbsp olive oil

salt and black pepper, to taste

Directions:

Heat oil in a deep soup pot over medium-high heat. Add onion, garlic and paprika and sauté, stirring, for 2-3 minutes or until soft.

Add in tomatoes and vegetable broth. Cover and bring to the boil, then reduce heat to low and simmer, stirring, for 10 minutes.

Remove from heat and blend until smooth. Return to pan. Stir in Brussels sprouts. Cook for 15 minutes more. Season with salt and pepper before serving.

Potato, Carrot and Zucchini Soup

Serves 4-5

Ingredients:

4-5 medium potatoes, peeled and diced

2 carrots, chopped

1 zucchini, peeled and chopped

1 celery rib, chopped

3 cups water

3 tbsp olive oil

1 cup almond milk

½ tsp dried rosemary

salt, to taste

black pepper, to taste

a bunch of fresh parsley for garnish, finely cut

Directions:

Heat the olive oil over medium heat and sauté the vegetables for 2-3 minutes. Add in 3 cups of water and the rosemary and bring the soup to a boil then lower heat and simmer until all the vegetables are tender.

Blend in a blender until smooth. Add a cup of almond milk and blend some more. Serve warm, seasoned with black pepper and sprinkled with parsley.

Gazpacho

Serves 6-7

Ingredients:

2.25 lb tomatoes, peeled and halved

1 onion, sliced

1 green pepper, sliced

1 large cucumber, peeled and sliced

2 cloves garlic

salt to taste

4 tbsp olive oil

1 tbsp apple vinegar

to garnish

1/2 onion, chopped

1 green pepper, chopped

1 cucumber, chopped

Directions:

Place the tomatoes, garlic, onion, green pepper, cucumber, salt, olive oil and vinegar in a blender or food processor and puree until smooth, adding small amounts of cold water, if needed, to achieve desired consistency.

Serve the gazpacho chilled with the chopped onion, green pepper and cucumber.

Main Dishes

Easy Vegan Pizza

Serves: 4

Ingredients:

1 store-bought or homemade dough

1/3 cup onion, chopped

1/2 cup tomato sauce

1/2 cup olives, halved and pitted

1/2 cup vegan cheese

2 tbsp olive oil

1/2 tsp oregano

1 tsp dried basil

a bunch of rocket leaves, to serve

salt and black pepper, to taste

Directions:

Heat a large skillet on medium heat and sauté the onion for 4-5 minutes until slightly charred. Add in the oregano and basil and sauté for 5 minutes more. Season with salt and black pepper to taste.

Roll out dough onto a floured surface and transfer to a parchment-lined 12 inch round baking sheet or pizza stone.

Top it with fresh or canned tomato sauce, vegan cheese, the sautéed onion and the olives.

Bake for 25-30 minutes in a preheated to 450 F oven or until the crust is golden brown and the sauce is bubbly. Let rest for 5 minutes before cutting, garnish with rocket leaves and serve immediately.

Eggplant Stew

Serves 4

Ingredients:

2 medium eggplants, peeled and diced

1 cup canned tomatoes, drained and diced

1 zucchini, diced

9-10 black olives, pitted

1 onion, chopped

4 garlic cloves, chopped

2 tbsp tomato paste

1 cup canned tomatoes, drained and diced

1/2 cup parsley, chopped, to serve

3 tbsp olive oil

½ tsp paprika

salt and black pepper, to taste

Directions:

Gently sauté onions, garlic, and eggplants in olive oil on medium-high heat for 10 minutes. Add paprika and tomato paste and sauté, stirring, for 1-2 minutes.

Add in the rest of the ingredients. Cover and simmer on low-heat for 30-40 minutes. Sprinkle with parsley and serve.

Eggplant and Chickpea Stew

Serves 4

Ingredients:

2-3 eggplants, peeled and diced

1 onion, chopped

2-3 garlic cloves, crushed

8 oz can chickpeas, drained

8 oz can tomatoes, undrained, diced

1 tsp paprika

1/2 tsp cinnamon

1 tsp cumin

3 tbsp olive oil

salt and pepper, to taste

Directions:

Peel and dice the eggplants. Heat olive oil in a large deep frying pan and sauté onions and crushed garlic. Add paprika, cumin and cinnamon. Stir well to coat evenly. Sauté for 3-4 minutes until the onions have softened.

Add the eggplant, tomatoes and chickpeas. Bring to a boil, lower heat and simmer, covered, for 15 minutes, or until the eggplant is tender.

Uncover and simmer for a few more minutes until the liquid evaporates.

Green Pea Stew

Serves 5

Ingredients:

2 bags frozen green peas

4 tbsp sunflower oil

1 medium onion, finely cut

2 carrots, chopped

1 tsp paprika

½ cup of fresh dill, finely cut

4 cloves garlic

salt, to taste

Directions:

Sauté the finely chopped onion and carrots. Add the garlic, the paprika and the green peas and simmer with some warm water for 30 minutes.

Season with salt and black pepper to taste. When ready sprinkle with the finely cut dill.

Green Pea and Mushroom Stew

Serves 4

Ingredients:

1 cup green peas (fresh or frozen)

4 large white button mushrooms, sliced

3 spring onions, chopped

1-2 cloves garlic

4 tbsp vegetable oil

1/2 cup water

1/2 cup finely chopped dill

Directions:

In a saucepan sauté mushrooms, spring onions and garlic. Add in the green peas and stew for 5-10 minutes until tender.

When ready sprinkle with dill. Serve warm.

Leek Stew

Serves 5-6

Ingredients:

1 lb leeks, cut

4 tbsp sunflower oil

1/2 cup vegetable broth

2 tbsp tomato paste

salt to, taste

fresh ground pepper, to taste

Directions:

Carefully clean leeks; cut off the stemmy bottoms and the dark green leaves, leave only white and light green parts. Cut leeks lengthwise in quarters, then into about 1 inch squares.

Heat oil in a heavy wide saucepan or sauté pan; add leeks, salt, pepper, and stir over low heat for 5 minutes. Add vegetable broth and bring to a boil, cover, and simmer over low heat, stirring often, for about 10-15 minutes or until leeks are tender.

Add tomato paste, raise heat to medium, uncover and let juices reduce to about half.

Potato and Leek Stew

Serves 4

Ingredients:

12 oz potatoes

2-3 leek stems cut into thick rings

5-6 tbsp olive oil

1/2 cup parsley, finely cut

salt, to taste

Directions:

Peel the potatoes, wash them and cut them into small cubes. Slice the leeks. Put the potatoes and the leeks in a pot along with some water and the oil. The water should cover the vegetables.

Season with salt and bring to the boil then simmer until tender. Sprinkle with the finely chopped parsley.

Zucchinis and Rice

Serves 4

Ingredients:

2 lb small zucchinis, diced

1 spring green onions, finely chopped

3 tbsp olive oil

2 cups water

2 medium tomatoes, diced

1 cup rice

1 tsp salt

1 tsp paprika

1 tsp black pepper

2 ½ cups water

1/2 cup fresh dill, finely cut

Directions:

Sauté the spring onions in olive oil and a little water. Cover and cook until soft.

Transfer onions in a baking dish, add zucchinis, tomatoes, rice, salt, paprika, pepper and water. Mix well.

Cover with foil and bake in preheated to 350 F oven for 30 minutes, or until rice is done. Sprinkle with dill.

Spinach with Rice

Serves 4

Ingredients:

1.5 lb fresh spinach, washed, drained and chopped

1/2 cup rice

1 onion

1 carrot

7 tbsp olive oil

2 cups water

Directions:

Heat the oil in a large skillet and cook the onions and the carrot until soft. Add the paprika and the washed and drained rice and mix well.

Add two cups of warm water stirring constantly as the rice absorbs it, and simmer for 10 more minutes.

Wash the spinach well and cut it in strips then add to the rice and cook until it wilts. Remove from the heat and season to taste.

Vegetable Stew

Serves 6

Ingredients:

3-4 potatoes, peeled and diced

2-3 tomatoes, diced

1-2 carrots, chopped

1-2 small onions, finely chopped

1 zucchini, peeled and chopped

1 eggplant, chopped

1 celery rib, chopped

1/2 cup green peas, frozen

1/2 green beans, frozen

1/2 cup sunflower oil

1 bunch of parsley

1 tsp black pepper

1 tsp salt

Directions:

In a deep saucepan, sauté the finely chopped onions, carrots and celery in a little oil. Add in the green peas, green beans, black pepper and stir to combine.

Pour over 1 cup of water, cover and let simmer. After 15 minutes add the diced potatoes, the zucchini, the eggplant and the tomato pieces.

Transfer everything into an ovenproof casserole, sprinkle with parsley and bake for about 30 minutes at 350 F.

Rice Stuffed Bell Peppers

Serves 4

Ingredients:

8 bell peppers, cored and seeded

11/2 cups rice

2 onions, chopped

1 tomato, chopped

fresh parsley, chopped

3 tbsp olive oil

1 tbsp paprika

Directions:

Heat the oil and sauté the onions for 2-3 minutes. Add the paprika, the washed and rinsed rice, the tomato, and season with salt and pepper. Add ½ cup of hot water and cook the rice until the water is absorbed.

Stuff each pepper with the mixture using a spoon. Every pepper should be ¾ full.

Arrange the peppers in a deep oven proof dish and top up with warm water to half fill the dish. Cover and bake for about 20 minutes at 350 F.

Uncover and cook for another 15 minutes until the peppers are well cooked.

Stuffed Red Bell Peppers with Haricot Beans

Serves 5

Ingredients:

10 dried red bell peppers

1 cup dried white beans

1 onion

3 cloves garlic, cut

2 tbsp flour

1 carrot

1 bunch of parsley

1/2 cup crushed walnuts

1 tsp paprika

salt, to taste

Directions:

Put the dried peppers in warm water and leave them for 1 hour. Cook the beans.

Chop the carrot and the onion, sauté them and add them to the cooked beans. Add as well the finely chopped parsley and the walnuts. Stir the mixture to make it homogeneous.

Drain the peppers, then fill them with the mixture and place in a roasting tin, covering the peppers' openings with flour to seal them during the baking. Bake it for about 30 min. at 350 F.

Stuffed Grapevine Leaves

Serves 6

Ingredients:

1.5 oz grapevine leaves, canned

2 cups rice

2 onions, chopped

2-3 cloves garlic, chopped

1/2 cup of currants

half bunch of parsley

half bunch of dill

1 lemon, juice only

1 tsp dried mint

1 tsp salt

1 tsp black pepper

3 tbsp olive oil

Directions:

Heat olive oil in a frying pan and sauté the onions and garlic until golden. Add the washed and drained rice, the currants, dill and parsley. Pour half a cup of olive oil and lemon juice in it. Add the black pepper, dried mint, salt and stir well.

Place leaf on a chopping board, with the stalk towards you and the vein side up. Snip away any tough remnants of the vein. Place about one teaspoon of the filling in the center of the leaf and towards the bottom edge. Fold the bottom part of the leaf over the filling, then draw the sides in and towards the middle, rolling the leaf up. The vine leaves should be well tucked in, forming a neat parcel. The stuffing should feel compact and evenly distributed.

Cover the bottom of a pot with grapevine leaves and stand the stuffed vine leaf parcels, packing them tightly together, on top. Pour water some water, to just below the level of the stuffed leaves. Place a small, flat ovenproof dish upside down on top, in order to prevent scattering. Cover with a lid.

Bring to the boil, then reduce the heat and simmer for about an hour checking occasionally that the bottom of the pot does not burn. The liquid should be absorbed giving a lovely sticky finish to the stuffed leaves. Serve warm or cold.

Green Bean and Potato Stew

Serves 5-6

Ingredients:

2 cups green beans, fresh or frozen

2 onions, chopped

4 cloves garlic, crushed

1/3 cup olive oil

1 cup fresh parsley, chopped

1/2 cup fresh dill, finely chopped

3-4 potatoes, peeled and cut in small chunks

2 carrots, sliced

1/2 cup water

2 tsp tomato paste

salt and pepper, to taste

Directions:

Sauté the onions and the garlic lightly in olive oil. Add the green beans, and the remaining ingredients.

Cover and simmer over medium heat for about an hour or until all vegetables are tender.

Check after 30 minutes; add more water if necessary. Serve warm - sprinkled with the fresh dill.

Cabbage and Rice Stew

Serves 4

Ingredients:

1 cup long grain white rice

2 cups water

1 small onion, chopped

1 clove garlic, crushed

1/4 head cabbage, cored and shredded

2 tomatoes, diced

1 tbsp paprika

1/2 cup parsley, finely cut

2 tbsp olive oil

salt, to taste

black pepper, to taste

Directions:

Heat the olive oil in a large pot. Add the onion and garlic and cook until transparent. Add the paprika, rice and water, stir and bring to boil.

Simmer for 10 minutes. Add the shredded cabbage, the tomatoes, and cook for about 20 minutes, stirring occasionally, until the cabbage cooks down.

Season with salt and pepper and serve sprinkled with parsley.

Roasted Broccoli

Serves 4

Ingredients:

2 medium broccoli heads, cut into florets

4 garlic cloves, lightly crushed

1 tsp fresh rosemary

1/4 cup olive oil

1 cup grated vegan cheese

Directions:

In a deep bowl, combine olive oil, rosemary, garlic and vegan cheese together. Toss in broccoli and coat well.

Place in a baking dish in one layer and roast in a preheated to 350F oven for 20 minutes; stir and bake for 10 minutes more.

Rice with Leeks and Olives

Serves 4-6

Ingredients:

6 large leeks, cleaned and sliced into bite sized pieces (about 6-7 cups of sliced leeks)

1 large onion, cut

20 black olives pitted, chopped

1/2 cup hot water

1/4 cup olive oil

1 cup rice

2 cups boiling water

freshly-ground black pepper, to taste

Directions:

In a large saucepan, sauté the leeks and onion in the olive oil for 4-5 minutes. Cut and add the olives and 1/2 cup water.

Bring temperature down, cover saucepan and cook for 10 minutes, stirring occasionally. Add rice and 2 cups of hot water, bring to boil, cover and simmer for 15 more minutes, stirring occasionally.

Remove from heat and allow to 'sit' for 30 minutes before serving so that the rice can absorb any liquid left.

Rice and Tomatoes

Serves 6-7

Ingredients:

1 cup rice

1 large onion, chopped

1 tbsp paprika

1/4 cup olive oil

1 tsp summer savory

2 cups canned tomatoes, diced

or 5 big ripe tomatoes

½ cup fresh parsley, finely cut

1 tsp sugar

Directions:

Wash and drain the rice. In a large saucepan, sauté the onion in the olive oil for 4-5 minutes. Add paprika and rice stirring constantly until the rice becomes transparent.

Pour 2 cups hot water and the tomatoes. Mix well and season with salt, pepper, summer savory and a teaspoon of sugar to neutralize the acidic taste of the tomatoes.

Simmer over medium heath for about 20 minutes. When ready sprinkle with parsley and serve.

Roasted Cauliflower

Serves 4

Ingredients:

1 medium cauliflower, cut into bite sized pieces

4 garlic cloves, lightly crushed

1 tsp fresh rosemary

salt to taste

black pepper

1/4 cup olive oil

Directions:

Mix oil, rosemary, salt, pepper and garlic together. Toss in cauliflower and place in a baking dish in one layer.

Roast in a preheated oven at 350 F for 20 minutes; stir and bake for 10 more minutes.

Stuffed Cabbage Leaves

Serves 8

Ingredients:

20-30 pickled cabbage leaves

1 onion, diced

2 leeks stems, chopped

1 1/2 cup white rice

1/2 cup currants

1/2 cup almonds, blanched, peeled, and chopped

2 tsp paprika

1 tbsp dried mint

1/2 tsp black pepper

1/3 cup olive oil

salt, to taste

Directions:

Sauté the onion and leeks in oil for about 2-3 minutes. Add the paprika, the black pepper and the washed and drained rice and continue sautéing until the rice is translucent.

Remove from heat and add the currants, finely chopped almonds and the peppermint. Add salt only if the cabbage leaves are not too salty.

In a large pot place a few cabbage leaves on the base. Place a cabbage leaf on a large plate with the thickest part closest to you. Spoon 1-2 teaspoons of the rice mixture and fold over each edge to create a tight sausage-like parcel. Place in the pot, making two or three layers of sarmi. Cover with a few cabbage leaves and pour over some boiling water so that the water level remains lower than the top layer of cabbage leaves. Top with a small dish upside down to prevent scattering.

Bring to the boil then lower the heat and cook for around 40 minutes. Serve warm or at room temperature.

New Potatoes with Herbs

Serves 4-5

Ingredients:

2 lb small new potatoes

1 tbsp mint

5 tbsp olive oil

1 tbsp finely chopped parsley

1 tbsp rosemary

1 tbsp oregano

1 tbsp dill

1 tsp salt

1 tsp black pepper

Directions:

Wash the young potatoes, cut them in halves if too big, and put them in a baking dish.

Pour the olive oil over the potatoes. Season with the herbs, salt and pepper.

Bake for 30-40 minutes at 350 F.

Orzo with Zucchinis

Serves 4-5

Ingredients:

1 cup orzo

2-3 medium zucchinis, cubed

1/2 onion

1/2 cup white wine

4 tbsp olive oil

1 tbsp dried oregano

1/3 cup fresh dill, finely cut

2 tbsp fresh squeezed lemon juice

1 tsp salt

1 tsp fresh black pepper

Directions:

Cook the orzo according to package directions (in salted water) and rinse thoroughly with cold water when you strain it. Place in a bowl, stir in two tablespoons olive oil, and set aside.

Gently sauté the onion and zucchinis in 2 tbsp of olive oil , stirring, until the onions are translucent. Add in oregano and white wine and cook uncovered on low heat for 10 minutes. Add in orzo and stir to combine well.

Add lemon juice, dill, and simmer, covered for 5 more minutes.

Breakfasts and Desserts

Avocado, Lettuce and Tomato Sandwiches

Serves: 2

Ingredients:

4 slices wholewheat bread

1 tbsp vegan basil pesto

2 large leaves lettuce

1/2 tomato, thinly sliced

1/2 avocado, peeled and sliced

6 slices cucumber

Directions:

Spread pesto on the four slices of bread.

Layer two slices with one lettuce leaf, two slices tomato, two slices avocado and three slices cucumber.

Top with remaining bread slices. Cut the sandwiches in half and serve.

Avocado and Chickpea Sandwiches

Serves: 4

Ingredients:

4 slices rye bread

1/2 can chickpeas, drained

1 avocado

2-3 green onions, finely chopped

1/2 tomato, thinly sliced

1/3 tsp cumin

salt, to taste

Directions:

Mash the avocado and chickpeas with a fork or potato masher until smooth. Add in green onions, cumin and salt and combine well.

Spread this mixture on the four slices of bread. Top each slice with tomato and serve.

Hummus Zucchini Toast

Serves: 2

Ingredients:

4 tbsp hummus

4 tbsp shaved zucchini

2 tbsp roasted salted sunflower seeds

2 slices crusty white bread, lightly toasted

Directions:

Toast 4 slices of white bread until golden.

Spread hummus onto each slice of bread; top with zucchini and sunflower seeds. Season with salt and pepper to taste, and serve.

Apple Cake

Serves: 12

Ingredients:

4-5 medium apples, sliced, cooked and mashed

1 cup walnuts, chopped

1/2 cup apple cider

1/2 cup sunflower oil

3 1/2 cups flour

1 1/2 cups sugar

1 tbsp baking powder

1/2 tsp baking soda

a pinch of salt

1 tsp cinnamon

1 /2 tsp fresh ground cardamom

1/2 tsp ground cloves

Directions:

Combine flour, baking powder, baking soda and salt. In another bowl, mix sugar, vegetable oil and apple cider, until well blended. Add in spices and stir to.

In a smaller bowl, mash the cooked apples. Add them to the other liquid ingredients and mix well. Add dry ingredients to wet ingredients. Stir until just combined. Add walnuts and stir again.

Spread batter evenly in a lined 9×13″ baking pan. Bake in a preheated to 350 F oven for 25 minutes. When completely cooled, dust with powdered sugar and cut.

Pumpkin Baked with Dry Fruit

Serves: 5-6

Ingredients:

1.5 lb pumpkin, cut into medium pieces

1 cup dry fruit (apricots, plums, apples, raisins)

1/2 cup brown sugar

Directions:

Soak the dry fruit in some water, drain and discard the water. Cut the pumpkin in medium cubes.

At the bottom of an ovenproof baking dish arrange a layer of pumpkin pieces, then a layer of dry fruit and then again some pumpkin. Add a little water.

Bake for 25-30 minutes at 350 F until the pumpkin is golden and there is no more water left. When almost ready sprinkle with sugar. Serve warm or cold.

Pumpkin Pastry

Serves: 8

Ingredients:

14 oz filo pastry

14 oz pumpkin

1 cup walnuts, coarsely chopped

1/2 cup sugar

6 tbsp sunflower oil

1 tbsp cinnamon

1 tsp vanilla

1/3 cup powdered sugar

Directions:

Grate the pumpkin and steam it until tender. Cool and add the walnuts, sugar, cinnamon and vanilla.

Place a few sheets of pastry in the baking dish, sprinkle with oil and spread the filling on top.

Repeat this a few times finishing with a sheet of pastry. Bake for 20 minutes at medium heat. Let the Pumpkin Pie cool down and dust with the powdered sugar.

Apple Pastry

Serves 8

Ingredients:

14 filo pastry

5-6 apples, peeled and diced

11/2 cup walnuts, coarsely chopped

2/3 cup sugar

6 tbsp sunflower oil

1 tbsp cinnamon

1/2 tsp vanilla extract

1/3 cup powdered sugar

Directions:

Cut the apples in small pieces and mix with the walnuts, sugar, cinnamon and vanilla.

Place two sheets of pastry in the baking dish, sprinkle with oil and spread the filling on top. Repeat this a few times finishing with a sheet of pastry.

Bake for 20 minutes at medium heat. Let the Apple Pastry cool down and dust with the powdered sugar.

Granny's Vegan Cake

Serves 12

Ingredients:

1/2 cup sugar

1 cup fruit jam

1 cup cool water

1/2 cup vegetable oil

1 cup crushed walnuts

1 tsp baking soda

21/2 cups flour

1 tsp vanilla powder

½ tsp cinnamon

Directions:

Combine the baking soda with the jam and leave for 10 min. Add sugar, water, oil, walnuts and flour in that order.

Mix well and pour in a round 10 x 2-inches cake pan. Bake in a preheated to 350 F oven. When ready turn over a plate and sprinkle with powdered sugar.

About the Author

Vesela lives in Bulgaria with her family of six (including the Jack Russell Terrier). Her passion is going green in everyday life and she loves to prepare homemade cosmetic and beauty products for all her family and friends.

Vesela has been publishing her cookbooks for over a year now. If you want to see other healthy family recipes that she has published, together with some natural beauty books, you can check out her Author Page on Amazon.

15843103R00051

Printed in Great Britain
by Amazon